Astrology and Zodiac Signs

The ultimate guide to Astrology, Zodiac signs, what they mean, Horoscopes, and more!

Table of Contents

Introduction	1
Chapter 1: What Is Astrology?	2
Chapter 2: What Are Zodiac Signs?	4
Chapter 3: The Signs and Their Meaning	6
Chapter 4: Horoscopes And How Do They Work?	14
Chapter 5: Creating The Horoscopes	18
Chapter 6: Astrology and Horoscopes Practical Applications	22
Conclusion	26

Introduction

I want to thank you and congratulate you for downloading the book, "Astrology and Zodiac Signs'.

This book contains helpful information about Astrology, what it is, and how it works!

Astrology is in fact a science, and can be a lot more complicated than what you may think based on the horoscopes you see in magazines.

This book will teach you how exactly Astrology works, including its ancient origins, the different zodiac signs, what they mean, the houses, the planets, and how they all relate to one another!

You will soon learn how to understand your own horoscope, and work out where your strengths, weaknesses, and opportunities lie.

This book will explain to you tips and techniques that will allow you to successfully understand and begin using astrology and zodiac signs in your life. Using this power of astrology can result in increased success in finance, relationships, your career, and more!

Thanks again for downloading this book, I hope you enjoy it!

Chapter 1: What Is Astrology?

The celestial bodies have always inspired awe and wonder in mankind. If we look to our past, many civilizations relied on it for a number of different and often important reasons. To turn skyward is to look divinity in the face, so to speak. For our ancestors, this cosmic dance correlates to everyday human life. Astrology is the study of these relationships and patterns; of the planets in motion and how it affects us according to our birth chart. What the horoscopes are and how it influences us; how it can help point us to find a better path and so on.

Astrology As A Form Of Science:

So, is Astrology a science? This is one of the most common questions that people ask when it comes to this particular branch of learning. It in fact falls under metaphysics or the study of things which are beyond the physical realm. It can be categorized with other fields of study which are based upon ancient theories. For example, you have feng shui, yoga as well as acupuncture. At its higher levels, astrology is basically the mastery of its particular scientific field. In fact, based upon its earliest known recording in history, it has been referred to as the "Mother of all Sciences".

The Theory and The Study:

There is no unified theory or practice when it comes to astrology. This is because different cultures have their own variations of it. Some of these have been combined to form what we know today as common western astrology. This isn't counting the eastern cultures that continue to practice their own form of it. Tibetan, Chinese and Vedic are among the most well-known when it comes to this group.

Let's talk western astrology. Within this sphere, there is a considerable amount of diversity when it comes to the philosophies as well as methods used. Shall we take a closer look?

- Mundane astrology: This is often used as a way of examining different world events. It can also be a way of predicting national affairs, the outcome of a war or the possible future of an economy.

- Interrogatory astrology: This generally refers to the use of astrology when it comes to making specific predictions about a particular subject's objectives. It can also be used to make an analysis of the different events that happen in their lives, aiding them in making tough decisions.

- Natal astrology: This is the kind of astrology that most people would be familiar with. It seeks to make analysis as well as predictions based upon the person's date of birth-- their zodiac sign. It is based upon the Law of Beginnings which states that: *Everything that happens to something is often also expressed at the very beginning of that thing.*

Chapter 2:
What Are Zodiac Signs?

By now, just about everyone has heard of the zodiac signs and most of them would have found out about them through horoscope columns in magazines or online. In these columns, the signs are often taken as major factors or determinants when it comes to a person's personality. However, this isn't the actual case when it comes to proper natal astrology. You might be surprised at how modest it can actually be.

These zodiac signs are considered as factors that color or modify the energies of the different major planets. It brings out certain traits related to it, while inhibiting others-- but without completely changing the planet's overall energy. Astrologers also tend to see the zodiac as an archetype of cyclic time, with the signs acting as different levels or phases in the development of the cycle itself.

So what exactly is the zodiac?

To put things more simply, if you observe the motion of the sun for an entire year, it would trace a large circle in our sky. This is what we refer to as "ecliptic" and also happens to be the lane that our planet follows. The zodiac is the thin band on either side of this ecliptic. Even the word zodiac itself means "circle of life".

What are the zodiac signs?

The zodiac is represented by different animals and is divided into 12 signs, each 30 degrees long. The cycle begins with Aries which is at the top of the ecliptic where the sun is at during the first day of spring. Keep in mind that the 30 degree sections of the sky are actually spaces and not time.

More often than not, zodiac signs are confused with sun signs. So whenever a person says that they are a Leo, what they're actually trying to say is that they were born during that time of the year when the sun hits the zodiac sign of Leo. Here's an interesting fact: Our calendar is actually designed to follow the motions of the sun around the zodiac and because of this, the sun is located in Aries at almost the same time each year. Looking at it in this manner, the 12 sun signs are akin to the months of our calendar following the zodiac. However, unlike the zodiac, they represent time instead of space.

The 12 zodiac signs are:

Aries, Taurus, Gemini, Cancer, Leo, Virgo, Libra, Scorpio, Sagittarius, Capricorn, Aquarius and Pisces.

Each has its own glyph or symbol representing it, as well as a planetary ruler and sub-cycles which comprise its core meaning. Every sign is representative of a certain type of energy and personality as well.

Chapter 3:
The Signs and Their Meaning

Alright, so you now know a bit more about the zodiac signs and how they play into astrology but do you know what meaning they hold for you? To help you better understand things and to provide you with insight as to the symbolism behind it, here's a summary of all that you need to know when it comes to the zodiac signs:

- **Aries**

    Element: Fire

    Ruling Planet: Mars

    Symbol: The Ram

    The glyph itself is a giveaway as to the kind of personality this particular sign represents. With the horns showing, the ram is an adventurous, aggressive and tireless animal. The energy associated with it is both feisty yet assertive. Both of which are trademarks of the Aries person. Another popular interpretation for the glyph is that it shows the eyebrows as well as the nose of the human face. It is often said that the Aries rules the head-- thought of as being headstrong and often acts on impulse before giving the action any real thought. The first sign in the zodiac, child-like in the sense that it is always prepared to start new and begin an adventure.

- **Taurus**

    Element: Earth

    Ruling Planet: Venus

    Symbol: The Bull

    The Ancient Egyptians, The Chaldeans and The Greeks are all associated with the mythology of the bull-king. This is also why there is an abundant representation of the bull in various symbolism found throughout these ancient cultures. The glyph representing the Taurus mimics the round face as well as the upward curve of a bull's horns. In terms of personality, they are known to be quite stubborn and impossible to budge, possessive over their space, dangerous whenever triggered but at the same time, they can also be slow moving, lazy at times but sensual. Taureans are also often linked to being concerned with acquiring wealth for material security.

- **Gemini**

    Element: Air

    Ruling Planet: Mercury

    Symbol: The Twins

    Many are often fascinated with the symbol that represents Gemini. As a glyph, it is shown as two upright I's and appears much like the Roman numeral for two. As the symbol suggests, Gemini is a dual sign. Traditionally, it represented all forms of duality such as positive and negative, light and dark. Personality-wise, this applies as well. They are known to rapidly change in mood and their energy levels tend to fluctuate a lot. They are also very versatile creatures and are very communicative. However, it cannot be denied that due to their dual nature, those who are close with a Gemini might sometimes feel as if they are dealing with two very different people.

- **Cancer**

    Element: Water

    Ruling Planet: The Moon

    Symbol: The Crab

    The glyph presents two circles with tails which can be interpreted in two ways. The first of which would be the crab with its curving yet powerful claws. The other, a woman's breasts which symbolizes nourishment and motherhood both of which are primary concerns for the Cancerian. The crab could represent their tenacity and sidelong approach to challenges. The crab's hard shell and vulnerable interior are spot on when it comes to the Cancer personality. They are known to be emotional defensive and self-protective but are truthfully, soft on the inside.

- **Leo**

    Element: Fire

    Ruling Planet: The Sun

    Symbol: The Lion

    Its glyph shows a curving line which is representative of the lion's mane. The animal itself is a great icon for this fiery and sunny sign, many of its well-known characteristics are quite feline like as well. For example, the graceful and proud bearing, the playfulness, their sensuality and love of pleasure, their need for a long rest which would then be followed by non-stop activity. In anger, a Leo can certainly mimic the lion's intimidating roar. In fact, due to their dramatic nature, this is one way for them to let off some steam.

- **Virgo**

    Element: Earth

    Ruling Planet: Mercury

    Symbol: The Virgin

    The only female figure in the Zodiac and one of two single human figures in the group, it represents the maiden and is often associated with the Greek goddess Demeter and her Roman counterpart, Ceres. For it's glyph, the coiled "M" design is said to be an image of the intestines, the body part that is ruled by the sign. It can also be interpreted as the ovaries or the uterus. Virgo is associated with hygiene and health, as well as all forms of healing and service. A person born under this sign is usually concerned with their diet and tends to experience nervous indigestion whenever they are worried or upset over something.

- **Libra**

    Element: Air

    Ruling Planet: Venus

    Symbol: The Scales

    It's representative of balance and harmony. As the sun begins its journey along the sign of Libra, it happens during the autumn equinox which occurs in late September. This is also the time of the year when the day and night are equal in length. Librans tend to be very concerned with justice-- hence the scales in which evidence is weighed. However, people under the sign of Libra are also known for their indecisiveness which comes from their own innate desire to analyze and evaluate everything to be able to make a more balanced judgment.

- **Scorpio**

    Element: Water

    Ruling Planets: Mars and Pluto

    Symbol: The Scorpion and The Eagle

    The "M" shaped glyph with its arrowed tail is representative of the scorpion and the deadly sting that it carries in its tail. Often brooding and intense, Scorpios have a reputation for retribution and harboring ill feelings towards those who have done them wrong. This is what the tail represents and it is considered a part of their whole character. As for the eagle, it represents the higher nature of the sign, the one that is often concerned with rebirth as well as transformation through sexual love. It is also associated with their ability to make conscious decisions in rising above their issues such as destructive urges, jealousy and even resentment.

- **Sagittarius**

    Element: Fire

    Ruling Planet: Jupiter

    Symbol: A Centaur.

    Half man and half horse, with a bow and arrow in hand. The glyph is an arrow or in some cases, a bow and an arrow. The centaur is pictured as being restless and ready to gallop into battle, towards new horizons. Much like the main characteristics of the sign itself, Sagittarians are always gearing forward. However, they are also often philosophical and are capable of seeing the duality and paradox in things-- this is one of the most essential parts of their personality.

- **Capricorn**

    Element: Earth

    Ruling Planet: Saturn

    Symbol: The Sea Goat.

    This mythical creature bears the upper body of a goat and tail of a fish. As for the sign's glyph, it resembles the letter "V" and is representative of the horns on the goat's head and curls downward to show the fish's tail. In mythology, there have been a number of sea gods who rule in the different realms of the ocean. For the seagoat, they are said to bring spiritual wisdom whenever it comes up on land - the same wisdom that is needed for practical tasks and the need to build. Capricorn is quite the ambitious sign and they have a profound understanding of the fact that merely satisfying one's ego is never genuinely fulfilling.

- **Aquarius**

    Element: Air

    Ruling Planets: Saturn and Uranus

    Symbol: The Water Bearer.

The second and only other single human figure in the zodiac, he is pictured as a man carrying a large vessel from which water is pouring out into the land. The glyph for the sign is two wavy lines which are parallel to each other. This represents water or electricity which is a nod to the sign's second planetary ruler, Uranus. Aquarius is an intellectual sign, often analyzing, thinking and talking about everything. They can also be emotionally detached but do carry strong feelings when it comes to human rights and justice. The water pouring out of the jar is a symbol of communication as well as the endless originality and mental energy that is essential to the Aquarian's character.

- **Pisces**

    Element: Water

    Ruling Planets: Jupiter and Neptune

    Symbol: The Two Fishes which are joined together but swim in directions opposite of each other.

Much like Gemini, Pisces is a dual sign and the fishes represent a lifelong battle that only Pisceans would understand. One of the fishes is swimming towards the more mystical and soulful ocean, completely intent on sacrificing itself for its beliefs (political, spiritual) as well as for the good of others. The other one is swimming toward self-fulfillment and achieving personal goals. The water surrounding the fishes represents the Piscean intuition and this helps them to make sense of the whole picture and balance their own inner struggle. Learning how to better trust others, while developing their intuition, is held in high regard by this sensitive yet complex sign.

Chapter 4:
Horoscopes And How Do They Work?

You might be familiar with what horoscopes are by now; after all, they are quite prevalent in many magazines. Whether you believe in them, take the words into consideration or simply find them entertaining, what you must know is that there is an actual science that goes into these things. It may not apply to magazine horoscopes but for astrologers, divining certain information from the positions of cosmic objects is certainly a science and an art.

But first, let's learn about the basics. *What is the horoscope exactly?*

The horoscope serves as a kind of diagram or stylized map of the heavens, showing a particular location at a certain moment in time; for example, a person's birth. In most of the applications it is used for, the perspective is geocentric--heliocentric astrology being the only exception. In the diagram, you'll find the positions of the actual planets along with the sun and moon. Together with these, you'll also see other purely calculated factors such as the house cusps, the mid-heaven, the zodiac signs, the ascendant, the lunar nodes and the lots.

In Western Astrology:

- The native would be what the event is about. A person's birth, for example. But it could also be the opening of a business, traveling and so on. This would be charted in it's particular time and place in the horoscope and is seen as the center of the celestial sphere.

- The celestial sphere would be the imaginary sphere in the diagram wherein the zodiac, planets and constellations are being projected on.

- The plane of the equator is basically the earth's equator projected into space.

- The plane of the ecliptic. This would be defined by the orbits of both the sun and earth. For practicality, both the plane of the equator and the plane of the ecliptic keep a constant 23.5 degree inclination to each other.

- The plane of the horizon is centered on the native. It is also tangential with the earth in that particular point. If placed within a sphere that has an infinitely large radius, this plane can be treated as an equal to the parallel plane with its center matching that of the Earth's. This should help in simplifying the basic geometry of the horoscope, however, it doesn't take into consideration that the native is in motion.

The Four Primary Angles of The Horoscopes:

- First house (Ascendant)

- Tenth House (Midheaven)

- Seventh House (Descendant)

- Fourth House (Imum Coeli or I.C.)

The ascendant refers to the sunrise point where the horizon and ecliptic intersect. This, along with the midheaven, is considered to be the most important angle within the horoscope. In many different styles of house division, the ascendant is often the cusp of the first house and the midheaven would be the cusp of the tenth house. Another thing that's considered to be significant would be the placement of the ascendant's planetary ruler; this is what's often referred to as the chart ruler.

As for your descendant, this would be the point in the west that's diametrically opposing the ascendant. It is normally the cusp of the seventh house and also opposes the M.C. Cusp of the fourth house which is the Imum Coeli or the northernmost point of your horoscope.

In creating a horoscope, the ascendant would be typically located at the nine o'clock position, on the left hand side of your diagram. There are rectangular versions of a horoscope chart and if you have that, there's no need to follow this step. Now, during the course of an entire day and because the Earth rotates, the entire ecliptic would actually pass through the ascendant and will advance by at least 1 degree. This movement is what provides us with a "rising sign" which is basically the sign of the zodiac that is currently rising over the eastern horizon during the moment of a person's birth. The point on the ecliptic which is further above the horizon is what's referred to as medium heaven and is located at the twelve o'clock position, where the sun is at if the person's birth time was during midday.

Houses:

In a horoscope, the houses refer to the series of twelve divisions that you'll be able to find on the plane of the ecliptic. Many astrologers have created differing ways of calculating these house divisions. When it comes to the equal house system, the ecliptic would be divided into the twelve equal houses which makes it about 30 degrees each. The first house would begin at the ascendant while the others would come counterclockwise starting from that point. The first six should come below the horizon while the other six would be above it. The positions of these houses will remain fixed in relation to the native. In this manner, the signs and planets would move through all of the twelve houses during the twenty-four hours of the day and the planets would follow the same motion but throughout the course of a month or a year.

Chapter 5:
Creating The Horoscopes

It's easy to think that horoscopes are created without any real science or logic behind them; that many of them are rehashed and are random thoughts put together by the so-called astrologers that write them. However, this is not always the case. While there are instances where this does happen, proper astrology certainly requires more than just random thoughts and lazy writing. There is a real science and art that goes into creating a horoscope.

Shall we get started?

In creating a horoscope, the astrologer would need to ascertain the exact place and time of the person's birth (or the initiation of an event if it's for something else). The local standard time (which might need adjusting for war time or daylight saving time) would then be converted into Universal time at the same instant. After this, the astrologer would then need to convert this into local sidereal time at the person's birth in order for them to be able to calculate both the ascendant and midheaven.

It is at this point that the astrologer would take an ephemeris, basically a table that lists the location of the planets, sun and moon for any given sidereal time, date and year with respect to the fixed stars (the northern hemisphere vernal equinox). Of course, this also depends upon which astrological system they are using. From this, the astrologer would then need to add or subtract the difference between the longitude of Greenwich as well as the longitude of the area in question in order to determine the true local mean time or LMT at the person's place of birth. Doing this would show where the planets would have been visible at that exact moment. Any planets that may have been hidden from view are also shown in the horoscope.

The horoscope would feature 12 different sectors located around the radius of the ecliptic, which begins from the eastern horizon with the rising sign. These 12 sectors, as you may have already figured out, are the houses or the twelve divisions located on the ecliptic plane. But what purpose do they serve in creating a horoscope?

The horoscope chart thus begins with this framework of 12 different houses. Over this, the signs of the zodiac would be superimposed. Using the equal house system, the cusp between the houses would fall at the same degree; twelve degrees for Leo, twelve degrees for Virgo and so on. For house systems that take into account any effects that the angle of intersection between planes of the horizon and the ecliptic might have, the calculations tend to become more complicated. For beginners, sticking to the equal house system would be the safest and easiest way to get started.

Placement Of The Planets:

Once the astrologer has managed to establish the positions of the signs in each respective house, they would then need to position the planets, sun and moon in their appropriate celestial longitudes. There are some astrologers who would take note of small planetary bodies such as asteroids and fixed stars along with some other mathematically calculated angles and points such as the equatorial ascendant etc. You can do this too but again, it might get complicated and confusing if this is your first time trying to create a horoscope.

Completing The Horoscope:

In order to complete the horoscope, the astrologer would have to take into account all of the aspects as well as relative angles between planetary pairs. The more exact aspects are considered to be of higher significance than the others. Understandably so, of course. The difference between an exact aspect and an actual aspect is referred to as an orb and the ones which are recognized by most astrologers include:

Conjunction (0 degree), Opposition (180 degrees), Trine (120 degrees), Square (90 degrees), Sextile (60 degrees), Sequisquare (135 degrees), Semi-square (45 degrees) and Quincunx (150 degrees).

These aspects are considered to work within a particular orb of influence and that the size of which would vary in relation to its importance. Modern astrologers, or at least most of them, would use an orb of 8 degrees or less for any aspects that involve the Moon, Sun and Jupiter then use smaller orbs for the other points.

What Purpose Does The Ascendant Have?

The Ascendant or ASC is a particular point on the ecliptic which rises in the eastern horizon during sunrise and undergoes changes while the earth continues to rotate within its axis. The ascendant plays an important role when it comes to astrological chart interpretation and exerts more power than the planets, sun and moon because of the fact that it actually influences every little thing in the natal chart.

The ascendant is also the first point of energy that you'll find in the natal chart, it is representative of how a person views life itself. The sign found on the ascendant shows how we express who we are as a person whenever we're dealing with other people as well as our first reactions when dealing with daily concerns. The longitude is important for determining the position of the ascendant because horoscopes do make use of local time. Once an astrologer finishes construction of the horoscope that they need, the task of interpreting the chart begins. All of which starts with the ascendant.

Chapter 6:
Astrology and Horoscopes Practical Applications

If you're keen on learning more about how to do astrology for yourself, there are easy ways through which you can get started. You already know how the zodiac and horoscopes work so all you need is a simple to follow guide on performing a "reading" for yourself. Here's how:

- First, you need a copy of your birth chart. This is a diagram that would show you the positions of the planets during the time you were born. It will become the fundamental basis for what you're about to do and is an important tool for astrology. There are numerous ways of getting this for yourself but the easiest would be going online and choosing a website that offers free chart calculation. Once you have your chart, do get familiar with it and find all the different positions that were mentioned in the previous chapters. Doing this should make the following steps much easier.

Now, you must also know what the different things on the chart represent:

- The Sun. This shows all of our deepest life goals and what we really want.

- The Moon. This shows the way we respond emotionally to what occurs around us. Our innermost feelings.

- Mercury. This shows us how we think as well as how we express ourselves.

- Venus. This shows us the way we relate with other people.

- Mars. This shows us how we make use of our talents and energy in order to achieve our goals.

- Jupiter. This shows us how we have fun and enjoy ourselves, as well as how we're able to expand our understanding further.

- Saturn. This shows us just how much self-discipline we have along with the strength of our character.

- Uranus. This shows us just how unique we are as well as how creative and inventive we can be.

- Neptune. This shows us the ways through which we can best use our energy for helping others.

- Pluto. This shows us the different ways we can grow as people if we simply choose to deepen our self-knowledge.

Learning about astrology and getting a better understanding of your horoscope can certainly help you in learning more about yourself - as well as about the people around you. It can help you learn of better ways of dealing with certain personalities and even give you certain advantages as well. Personally, you'll find that it can provide you with some insight into your future and what you can do to make it even better. Information about your career, relationships, romance, finance, family and health along with other aspects of your life can be divined through it.

Different Ways That Knowing About Horoscopes Can Help:

- Find your innate strengths and talents. This can certainly serve as an advantage for you once you become more aware of what you can be capable of. Most people tend to discover these things way later in life or not at all. In knowing about it early on, you have more time to hone it and utilize it to its maximum potential.

- Helps you become more aware of your deficiencies and weaknesses. In finding out what sort of things you're good at, you'll also learn about the problem areas where you might need some improvement. This is another important factor when it comes to developing as a person.

- Need a bit of help when it comes to decision making? Horoscopes can help you ascertain the success rate and future prospects that a particular decision can provide you with. From there, you can weigh your options and choose the right one for yourself and your future. We all need a little push every now and then, right?

- Gives you insight into how other people might act or think. While it may not always be spot-on, this can still give you a bit of an edge especially if you're in a field where a talent for interacting with people is highly valued. Find out what they might be interested in, if you'll be compatible as friends or co-workers with them as well as a few other personality traits.

- The above also applies to romantic relationships. Whilst you shouldn't let your horoscope completely influence your decisions when it comes to these matters, that little bit of insight can certainly help you in getting to know a potential partner more.

However, it is also important for you to remember that you're still the designer of your own future. Take what the horoscopes provide as a kind of guide and make better choices using the insight it has given you. Don't let it influence everything you do; every thought and every decision that you make because that is not what it was meant for. Always practice common sense.

Conclusion

Thank you again for downloading this book!

I hope this book was able to help you learn more about Astrology!

The next step is to put this information to use, and begin using the power of astrology and zodiac signs to understand your horoscope and enhance your future!

Finally, if you enjoyed this book, please take the time to share your thoughts and post a review on Amazon. It'd be greatly appreciated!

Thank you and good luck!

www.ingramcontent.com/pod-product-compliance
Lightning Source LLC
LaVergne TN
LVHW021748060526
838200LV00052B/3534